FOR LITTLE LIVES

A Collection of God's Truths Revealed
Through Parenting

By

Maggie Adkinson

For Little Lives: A Collection of God's Truths Revealed Through Parenting

This book is a work of love. The stories are based on the author's life experiences. All personal experiences mentioned are based on true stories and used for educational content, humor, and impact.

Thank you to Sarah for all your support, proofreading, honesty, and friendship. Thank you to Stephanie for your editing skills. Author photograph by Amy Beckling Photography.

ISBN: 978-1-62888-781-5
FCI Publications
First Edition: January 2022

Table of Contents

Introduction

As a little girl, I played house all the time. I remember rolling up socks and putting them in my undershirt to create a womanly figure.' I carried my dolls around, dressing and nursing them all day long. As a teenager, I babysat and corralled the neighborhood kids together to play games. I knew from a young age that I wanted to be a mom.

As I got older, the desire to be a mom grew. I was drawn to every baby I saw and dreamed of the day I would be married and have my own family. I longed to hold my own baby in my arms, to smell that new baby smell, and to watch them grow up.

I was what you might call a late bloomer in the marriage department. I didn't meet my husband until I was 29, but in less than a year, we were married. We both knew that we wanted to have a family, so it wasn't long before we started trying. And we tried an awful lot for a long time.

After a year of trying, we started talking to doctors. We were put on the prescription sex plan—that's what we called it. You mark your calendar for a day and time, and you make sure it happens. It took most of the joy out of it, but we wanted a family, so we got busy.

Another year passed, and we were still missing one of the two little blue lines. I can't even remember how many negative pregnancy tests I saw. And if I did remember the number, it would probably shock us all. So, we went to more doctors. And had more tests done. And then we got the phone call.

"You have a zero percent chance of becoming pregnant. There are no treatments that will change this."

At that moment, my heart and dreams were shattered. A decade later, I still find tears streaming down my face thinking of that conversation and the emotions that collided into me.

Then I had to share that news with my husband. He got home from work, and we sat on the end of the bed. With wreaking sobs, I told him what I had not yet grasped. Together we cried out every dream, hope, and vision for what we thought our future would be.

Two years later, we found ourselves in another doctor's office waiting for more news that would change our lives. But this time, we were waiting to see a heartbeat of the baby that we thought we would never have. In those two years, God moved in our hearts, especially mine, and drew us into the world of adoption. In that journey alone, we had a lot of ups and downs. After a last-minute failed adoption, we redirected our focus and decided to adopt embryos.

If you're not familiar with this process, it's fascinating. Many families go through fertility treatments and find themselves with embryos—little, tiny, microscopic people—that they don't want or need. It's then they need to decide what to do with them. Some of the most common choices are to keep them frozen with no plan, destroy them or donate them to science. Another option, and newer at this time in our lives, is to donate them to an agency where another family can adopt them.

We chose our family out of a list of hundreds of options and had six embryos to work with. Six weeks before this appointment, we transferred two strong embryos into my uterus, and the waiting game was on. Six weeks. Not too long until you are waiting to see if you are a mom.

On this day, we sat in the office waiting to see if our dreams would be resurrected. My husband looked at me and said, "I'm so nervous you couldn't get a ten-penny nail up my butt crack." He can always bring humor to a tense situation. But then we saw our dreams come true. We saw not just one, but two tiny little heartbeats flickering on the screen.

And our lives have not been the same.

Parenthood—it changes you.

Suddenly, I needed loaded cheese fries every other day, I hated the smell of coffee, and I found myself crying with every exaggerated emotion I had. Our bathroom counters were covered with injections to help my body support these babies that we didn't conceive. My phone was filled with reminders to take medications and give myself shots so our babies would continue to grow. The couch had a garbage can next to it and all the parenting books on it. Already our lives were changed.

And then these little babies were born. They were tiny and perfect, and they were ours. The love that we felt for them up to that point became a drop in the ocean. I didn't know and was unable to understand before then the emotions that would come with these tiny babies.

Twenty months later, we found ourselves with another set of twins, and we were drastically outnumbered. Four kids under the age of two! That's about all I remember from that year. After we survived the first year with our two sets of twins, we settled into a chaotic and crazy life.

Becoming a mom has been one of the most spiritually transformative things in my life. And it's not a one-time thing. It's ongoing. It happens every day if I allow the Holy Spirit to reveal things to me. I will never be the same again.

It's only when we choose God over ourselves that we become transformed in our view of God. When we look into our child's eyes, we can begin to understand God's love for us. When our children are hurting, we understand how God gave everything, even His only Son, because He loves us, because we would do anything for our children.

I have been given the most amazing little boys to parent. I have the privilege to guide, support, love, nurture, and mold these little lives. It's not easy, and I'm not doing it perfectly. But some days, I do it right. Some days I see a glimpse of great things, a small reward in comparison to the challenges.

It's on these days that I am also reminded that I am a broken person living a sinful life in a broken world. But the grace and love of God abounds.

This book is a collection of things God has reminded me of while teaching my boys. Sometimes they are simple and basic. Others are deeply powerful moments for me. (Times when God is calling me to go deeper in my faith, my marriage, my parenting, or so many other areas where I am lacking.) It's in these moments that I am thankful for the loving presence of God that gently—or not so gently—prods me in the direction of truth and obedience.

My hope is that as you read this book, you can laugh at my mishaps and walk a little closer to God. My family is crazy, and my life is a non-stop adventure. Thank you for joining me on this ride.

PART I: Friendship

Chapter One: Lonely In the Midst of a Crowd

A few weeks ago, one of the boys had a friend come over to play. Leading up to this event, all they talked about was how excited they were that he was coming. They followed me around the house for days saying, "I can't wait for Ryan to come to my house to play" and "I'm so excited for my friend Ryan to come."

The day and hour came, and you would have thought it was an early Christmas present. Ryan came in the house . . ., but nothing changed. They still followed me around the house, talking about how excited they were that Ryan came to play.

They didn't play with Ryan. They didn't talk to Ryan. They just talked about Ryan being at our house. They talked about their friend instead of enjoying the time of being with their friend.

While I don't think my boys would say they were lonely that day, it made me wonder a bit. What are we looking for? We look forward to having friends. We long for deep and connected friendships. But, in the crowd, sometimes we may miss what we have right in front of us.

It's hard to admit, but sometimes, I'm lonely. It's so hard, in fact, that I have put off writing this for a long time. I have friends. Good friends. Casual friends. Situational friends. Family friends. Girlfriends. Spiritual friends. I would even say I have a lot of friends.

But sometimes I'm lonely.

I recently read a book, and one section resonated with me in very deep ways.

"These days, loneliness is the new cancer—a shameful, embarrassing thing, brought upon yourself in some obscure way. A fearful, incurable thing, so horrifying that you dare not mention it; other people don't want to hear the word spoken aloud for fear that they might too be afflicted, or that it might tempt fate into visiting a similar horror upon them."[1]

I understand how Eleanor felt this way. I don't want to share my loneliness because I don't know how people will respond to this "affliction," and I fear that I am the only one with this "sickness."

Some of my loneliness is self-imposed. I think I need to do things on my own so I don't ask or invite people to join me. I don't want to be a burden to others. I don't want to appear needy. I don't want to be that pushy friend that makes you cringe when you see a call from them. I don't want people to have to make excuses not to get together, so I just don't ask.

But truthfully, when I do reach out, the response is love and friendship.

Some of my loneliness is a product of the season of life I'm in. I have four kids under the age of five, I'm a stay-at-home mom, and I homeschool. All of that adds up to being remarkably busy for me. With naps thrown in, I have little spare time to connect with friends or pour into relationships.

And some of my loneliness is perception. Everyone I see has lots of friends already. They don't need or want more—especially me. But is that true? I don't think so. (At least I don't think so.) When I talk to a new friend (maybe someone I just met or an

---

[1] Honeyman, *Eleanor Oliphant Is Completely Fine*, p. 227.

acquaintance I'm getting to know better), they respond with kindness and welcoming acceptance.

Overstated topic, but I think it needs to be said—social media doesn't help our perceptions. We see groups of people together and notice that we aren't invited. We see tagged posts, and our name isn't there. It just adds to a feeling of loneliness and not being included. We need to stop judging ourselves and our lives on the perception we have of other people.

Not everyone feels lonely like this. Some people are just natural at being friends with everyone. But for those of us who are introverts, we are not that way.

The day my boys had a friend over frustrated me. I don't know how many times I said, "Stop following me around and go play with your friend."

But I'm the same way. On a hard day, am I going to pick up my phone and let a friend know what's going on? Not very often. Why not? Pride. Fear. Insecurity. Aren't those from Satan? Isn't he trying to keep me isolated and away from friends who will encourage me and make me stronger?

Like my boys, sometimes I miss out on the friends that are right in front of me. I long for close friends to text and call. But when I text, they text back. When I call, they talk to me. When I need support, they give it. When I need help, they are there.

I won't ever be the person that has dozens of close friends. That's just not me. And that's OK. But I can be the person that reaches out when I feel Satan settling in. I can be the person that connects with others when I feel the Holy Spirit's nudge.

And this can be harder. I can be a person who celebrates all the relationships I have. I can be a person who scrolls through social media and celebrates your dinner party or play date and not feel lonely or less than. I can make a phone call every week. I can connect, in some way, with a friend every day. I can reach out to a new and developing friendship each week.

When I'm so absorbed in myself and what I don't have, I miss all that I do have. When I am waiting for someone to connect with me, I may miss out on the opportunity to encourage them by reaching out. Because truly, in the crowd, we can get lost. But when we look away from ourselves, just like my boys, we may have a friend right there.

Chapter Two: Comparison

I have a Facebook friend from a past life, and her life is perfect. She has lots of littles like me but seems to handle parenting with so much more grace, patience, and love than I can even attempt to muster. She's intentional with her time, and she's always giving with her love and only speaks kind words. Her kids are well-behaved, never sassy or whiney, and are always kind to strangers and puppies.

And we all know none of that is true. Right?

But it seems like she's got it all together, especially on the days when I'm losing it. Like last night at dinner, all four kids were screaming for different reasons. One didn't like what I made. One didn't want to eat the mandatory three bites. One just wanted to be held. And one cried because I looked at him wrong. And when I say cried, I really mean screamed.

When I look at my home and compare it to my friend's perfect Facebook life, I am a total mom failure.

But here's the truth: I'm only failing because I compared myself to someone else. And it's a comparison of what I think their life is like, not what it actually is.

I'm not a failure, and neither are you.

Sure, you may be better at some of these momming things than I am. But I bet I'm better than you at some things. And that doesn't make us failures. It makes us human. It means we need each other and God.

Because if I have it all together, why do I need anyone or anything else?

And here's the best part. These little people God has entrusted me with were chosen by God for me. It wasn't an accident; we chose them out of thousands of embryos. They weren't forgotten by God when they sat frozen for over seven years. It wasn't just luck that the transfers were successful.

No. These precious boys were chosen by God for me. Chosen by God!

(And just because you have a biological child doesn't mean they weren't chosen for you. Think of all the possibilities of little people that could have come about, but this is one that came to be!)

Because they were chosen *for* me, I am the best mom *for* them. Not some friend on Facebook or the mom at the playground. No matter how much those moms seem to have it together, they aren't the best for my boys. God chose best, and it's me.

So, in those moments when I want to compare myself to you, I'm going to remember that I cannot be you. I can only be me. And God chose me. Hebrews 12:1 says for us to "run with perseverance the race marked out for us" (*NIV*). God has already chosen a race for me and one for you. He chose me to run my race, not yours.

I am Maggie . . . wife . . . adoptive mom . . . daughter of the Most High God and I will work to be the best me that I can be.

Chapter Three: My Slippers

I absolutely love autumn and the entire season leading into Christmas. Pumpkin smells mixing with gingerbread and fresh pine! There is joy, love, generosity, excitement . . . so many great feelings and emotions that roll together to become something truly special.

One of my favorite things about that time of year is shopping for gifts. I love to find the perfect gift. I love to shop for an incredible deal. I love to wrap those gifts in beautiful paper.

But there is a danger in shopping for gifts and looking for the best deal—you realize everything you don't have. You find out that you need a lot of things that you never knew you needed. You get ads and catalogs showing you all the great stuff that is out there. And if you're like me, you recognize something that a friend has and think: "I'd like to have one of those." You may buy it; you may not. But the damage has been done. But, the comparison has been made.

My book club read the book "Cutting For Stone." There was a quote in this book that has really stuck with me. It won't leave. It rolls through my mind.

It's challenging.

It's convicting.

It's life-changing.

If I let it be.

"The key to your own happiness is to own your slippers, own who you are, own how you look, own your family, own the talents you have, and own the ones you don't also. . . . If you keep saying your slippers aren't yours, then you'll die searching, you'll die bitter, always feeling you were promised more."[2]

This quote continues to remind me to find satisfaction where I am. To be content with what I have. To enjoy who I am and how I look. To be thankful for what I have been blessed with.

If I start to look around, I may see that what I have is less desirable than what you have. But pursuing your happiness will not bring me happiness. I have my own slippers, and they may look dirty and scuffed up when I compare them to someone else, but they are mine, and they fit. Your slippers don't fit me. I can try to shove my foot in them, but they will only make me stumble.

What makes us happy, at our core, is so very personal. Your happiness is not my happiness. Your family is not my family. Your talents are not my talents. Search for what brings you joy. Search for happiness in your life. Find who you are and give thanks for what you have.

I have been communicating with a family that is serving on the mission field. I asked them what they missed most from America. Their response—goldfish and marshmallows. The simplicity of this response has settled deep in our family. I'm sure they could have said a million different things, but they knew what would make their family happy—smiling goldfish and marshmallows to roast over a fire.

Are my wants that simple? Or do I complicate them because of what I see around me?

Instead of comparing, let's live a life of thankfulness—a life of generosity.

---

[2] Verghese, *Cutting For Stone*, p. 351.

Let us focus on being thankful for the slippers we have. The talents we have. The family we have. And yes, even the things we don't have.

Let's find the simplicity of life with no comparison.

And let's give generously. Let's figuratively load up the mail with goldfish and marshmallows. Let's share and give in big and small ways.

That's when we will embrace what this season is about.

PART II: Parenting

Chapter Four: The Epic Tantrum

Today we went to the park to ride bikes and take a walk. All the walking and tree climbing resulted in sand inside the shoes of one of my precious littles. We stopped and dumped out the shoes. We brushed off stinky feet. And waited (and waited) for the shoes to be put back on. But it wasn't enough. Apparently, he is like the princess who feels a pea under dozens of mattresses. He felt that one grain of sand in his shoe, and it resulted in an epic temper tantrum. He wouldn't walk with us. He was about 30 steps behind, crying and yelling. The rest of us continued on our way.

As I approached the car, he stopped walking. He stood across a field watching me and crying his little heart out. He yelled for me. He stomped his feet. He cried. He called my name. (And peed his pants.) I sat down where I was in the grass and waited. Every few minutes, I would encourage him to walk to me, tell him I loved him, remind him that he was OK. And it didn't faze him. He still cried, stomped, and screamed.

There was a group of teenagers close by watching the whole thing go down. I heard them saying things like . . .

"Look at her; she's doing nothing."

'Is she leaving him?'

"She just sat down."

'Why won't she get him?'

And they were right, except about the leaving part. I sat there and let him cry. I let him scream. And then, suddenly (20 minutes later), it was over. He started walking toward me. I held out my arms, and he ran into them, wiping his snotty nose on his shirt. And I hugged him—covered in snot and pee. As he sniffled into my shirt, I reminded him of how he is loved. I reminded him that I am always there for him and that I will never, ever stop loving him.

Here's the thing. I can remember times, more than I want to admit, that I have stood away from God and stomped my feet. I have cried out to Him to come to me. And the whole time, He is just waiting for me to come to Him.

Maybe I ran away from Him. Maybe I allowed sin to get in the way of our relationship. Maybe I chose to ignore His voice. Maybe I just wanted to stomp my feet and cry because I didn't get what I wanted. And I wonder, how many times was that tantrum with God over something as small as a grain of sand in my shoe.

Watching my little guy today was heartbreaking. I wanted to go to him. And everyone around me wanted me to go to him. But I needed him to come to me. In the same way, I saw my little boy, God sees us.

One of my favorite names of God found in the Bible is El Roi, "the God who sees me." This name for God is found in Genesis 16. Hagar was given to Abraham to bear him a son. But when she conceived, Sarah was not happy. She treated Hagar so badly that Hagar ran away. When God appeared to her, she was alone in the wilderness. I'm sure she was scared, sad, angry, confused, and pregnant. Genesis 16:13 says, "She gave this name to the LORD who spoke to her 'You are the God who sees me,' for she said, 'I have now seen the One who sees me.'" (*NIV*)

God saw her in that moment. God saw her hurt and fears. God saw her after she ran away. And Hagar acknowledged that God saw her. Just like Hagar, God sees us exactly where we are. He knows exactly what is going on—in the present, the past, and the future.

- When we are hurting, God sees us.

- When we have run away from troubles brought on by our sinful choices, God sees us.

- When we are afraid, God sees us.

- When we are all alone in the wilderness, God sees us.

When we are far from God by choice, circumstance, or by perception, I believe God's heart is breaking. The question is not what brought us so far, but rather what will we do about it. Will we stand in the wilderness stomping our feet and crying? Or will we listen to God calling us home and run to Him? Because He is waiting. Luke 15:20 says, "But while he was still a long way off, his father saw him and was filled with compassion for him; he ran to his son, threw his arms around him and kissed him." (*NIV*)

While he was still a long way off … God sees us where we are, and as soon as we step toward Him, He sees it. His heart races, He smiles and holds out His arms to us.

Chapter Five: The Sweet Spot

"It goes so fast." "I can't believe they are already [insert age]." "How did this happen?" These are the responses I give when people comment on how old my kids are. But what I don't say is "time slow down."

I don't want time to slow down. I love parenting at every age. (Although three about sent me to the loony bin.)

- I loved holding my newborn and staring into his eyes.

- I loved nursing at 3 AM because it was our time and no one else's.

- I loved rocking him to sleep even when he should have been crying it out.

- I loved seeing him learn to crawl and walk and climb.

- I loved listening to him learn to talk.

- I loved watching his personality bloom.

- I loved having conversations with him and hearing what he thinks about life.

- I love it all.

And while I loved all of that, I don't want to go back to it. Not because I don't miss it, because I do miss newborn snuggles and a sleeping baby on my shoulder. I don't want to go back because I can't wait to see what's ahead.

- I want to see his first t-ball game.

- I want to see what his favorite subject is in school.

- I want to see his first crush.

- I want to be there after his first heartache.

- I want to teach him to drive.

- I want to see him go to prom, graduate from high school and go off to college.

- I want to see him fall in love, get married, and become a father.

- I want to see him fulfill God's plan for his life.

I don't want to live in the past and wish for those moments again. I'm not going to get them back. They will only live on as memories.

I don't want to live in the future and always wish for this stage to end. (Even the hard stages; if I look, there are sweet victories in them!) I don't want to push them too far or too hard.

I want to live in the present.

I want to embrace the dirty diapers, temper tantrums, fingerprints on the walls, and all of the other uncomfortable moments. Because with that, I will also embrace a little voice saying "mamaaaa" every time he sees me. I will enjoy the hugs and him telling me I'm "bootiful."

This is the moment I am in. It's hard and exhausting. But today is the only day they will be this age. Tomorrow they will be a day older. A day may not seem like much, but in one day, they learn to walk. In one day, dad is the new favorite. In one day, a lot can happen.

So today, I will love everything that happens. Today I will love my boys with my whole heart. Because tomorrow they will be different.

Time, don't slow down. Help me to appreciate each minute I've been given and to love being there.

Chapter Six: Adoption Is Hard

Adoption is close to my heart . . . for obvious reasons as that is how God formed our family. It's joyful. It's a time of celebration. It's a choice. You are choosing someone to be your family. Not by chance or luck . . . but an intentional, deliberate choice. Adoption is the beginning of a new life.

But with joy comes the pain of a loss—a death, so to speak. Every adoption is because there was a loss—a death of the past.

Death is always hard. Even the death of a painful past is hard. It requires acknowledgment of the past—a time of mourning. When you leave the past behind, you always wonder. And you always bring a piece of it with you into the future. Sometimes it's the pain. Sometimes it's the memories. Sometimes it's the scars, visible and hidden. But it's there.

My boys were adopted before they were even born. (Embryo adoption is so cool!) They don't know anything else. But they still have a past. They have a past life they will never know about. While I can't change their past, I can influence their future. While I can't take away the past—where they came from—I can pray they are protected from the hurt of that past.

And I do pray. I pray they can see that they were chosen. I pray they can see they are loved. I pray they will see that they are living out God's plan for their lives. And while it may not SEEM perfect at times, I pray they know it is perfect FOR THEM.

I know someday I will have to answer questions that I don't have answers to. I know someday I will hold them while they mourn the death of what they do not know and will never have. I don't understand the pain and loss of not knowing where you came from. But I can celebrate with them where they are going.

I know what the future holds because I have been adopted by Christ. When we are adopted into the family of God, there is a death to our old life. There are times that death reveals itself as scars or old wounds that need to be healed. But when we allow love, which is the foundation of every adoption, to be the catalyst for our future, the past isn't as important. We will remember it, but it won't define us.

So, while I celebrate my family's adoption and all adoptions, I am mindful of what lies below the surface. I pray for my children and every other adopted child to receive the healing and protection of the Spirit. And I pray they can find their true identity not in what was, but in what will be.

"He will wipe away every tear from their eyes; and there will no longer be any death; there will no longer be any mourning or crying or pain; the first things have passed away. And He who sits on the throne said, "Behold, I am making all things new." (*NIV,* Revelation 21:4-5)

Chapter Seven: Have Patience

There is a song I remember from when I was a little girl. The lyrics said, "Have patience. Don't be in such a hurry. When you get impatient, you only start to worry. Remember that God is patient too. Think of that when others have to wait on you."

I sing this song a lot at home because it so happens that I have four very impatient little boys that live with me. One asks for things incessantly without ever giving up. One jumps up and down and whines when he wants something. One squeals in frustration when he doesn't get what he wants. My final one just walks away saying, "o-tay." He is the easy-going one in the bunch.

But patience can be just as hard for me as it is for my littles. Sometimes I ask God for things again and again and again. Sometimes I stomp my feet because I haven't gotten what I asked for when I wanted it. And I have been known to scream or cry out in frustration when things don't happen the way I thought they should.

I've been working with my boys to have more patience. I'll tell them about something they can get or experience, but they have to wait. And wait patiently. That means not asking too often. That means not getting frustrated. That means hanging in there until they get what has been promised to them.

Sometimes they get the reward.

And sometimes they don't.

Some days they are examples of what patience looks like. And they get the cookie.

Other days, they just can't hang on. Sometimes it happens quickly. Other times they are so close to getting the reward, and then they lose it, figuratively and literally, and they don't get the cookie.

It's those moments that make me sad. They just missed it. If they had hung on a little longer, they would have gotten what was intended for them.

But I'm sure God is smiling to Himself when I am feeling sad for my boys. He's smiling because He knows exactly how I am feeling. He's smiling because He remembers the times when I gave up waiting for something just before He was going to give it to me. Not every time, but sometimes.

It reminds me of when Moses when to Mt. Sinai to meet with God. Exodus 24:15-16 says, "When Moses went up on the mountain, the cloud covered it, and the glory of the LORD settled on Mount Sinai. For six days, the cloud covered the mountain, and on the seventh day the LORD called to Moses from within the cloud." (*NIV*)

What if Moses had gotten tired of waiting on God. What if on the fifth day he said, "I'm done, God isn't coming, so I am leaving." He would have missed out on being in the presence of God. He would have missed out on what God had for Him. He would have missed out on the victories that God had in store. Moses spent six days in the waiting. I'm sure it was a long wait . . . with a lot of wondering.

I remember vividly the days of waiting to have a family. Days, weeks, and months of waiting on God to answer my prayers to be a mom. What if, in all the waiting, I just gave up waiting and moved on? I would have never explored adoption. What if, after our failed adoption, I threw in the towel because it was too painful? I wouldn't have met a friend who told me about embryo adoption. What if I didn't want to wait 18 months for an appointment? What if that was too long and daunting, and I gave up? I would have missed out on the four little people who call me mom.

Waiting is hard. But to give up waiting means I may miss what God is doing. He's not wasting my time or my hurt. Moses probably thought:

- What are you doing God?

- How long should I stay here?

- Where are you?

- Did you bring me here just to sit around?

- What's next?

So, do you find yourself waiting?

- Waiting for a victory in your marriage.

- Waiting for a positive pregnancy test.

- Waiting on a new job or for that big promotion.

- Waiting for financial freedom.

- Waiting to be free from depression.

- Waiting for deep friendships.

- Or maybe just waiting for something more.

Instead of focusing on the waiting, think of what victory you are on the cusp of seeing. It may be just around the corner. Don't stop waiting.

When it's hard. When it's scary. When you're unsure. When you're tired.

Don't stop. God is right there.

Chapter Eight: I'm Going to Keep You Forever

Today it happened. I knew it was coming. I was preparing myself for it. I was praying about it. I was thinking about it. But it still caught me off guard.

"What does adopted mean?"

I should have said . . .

. . . adopted means that you became part of a new family.

. . . when you are adopted, you gain all the rights and privileges of being a part of that family.

. . . it means you are chosen.

. . . when you are adopted, it means you are home.

But I didn't say any of that. I talked about how mama and daddy couldn't have a baby. I told him about his other mom and dad, and they loved him so much they gave him (and his brothers) to us. It was factual. It was uninteresting. It was blundered. Or so I thought until he said,

"Adopted means I'm going to keep you forever."

And that's it. Adoption means I'm going to keep you forever.

Son, I will keep you forever. You are mine, and I am yours.

What a great reminder that we are adopted by God. We gain all the privileges of being a child of God. We are co-heirs with Jesus. We were chosen by God. And one day, one glorious day, we will go home to live with Him forever.

We get to keep God forever.

Chapter Nine: Lukewarm

I am a home-school mom. We decided to give it a try for a few years and see how it goes. So far, just over a year in, we love it. I love seeing the boys get new concepts. I love the smile on their face when they read their first words. I love teaching them silly facts about dinosaurs and cowboys. I love the opportunity to pour into them in every area of their lives.

Those are the perfect days.

And they don't come around too often.

Most of the time, there is one person who is just going through the motions of school but not really trying. Being a perfectionist, seeing someone not do their best will wad up my panties. It's so frustrating. And I may tend to over-react a little in those moments.

One week I remember, was particularly bad. They couldn't tell me the name of any letter even though I knew they knew them. I got snippy; I raised my voice; I forced them to do the activity again and again and again even when I saw their frustration was increasing along with mine. Finally, I threw the cards down on the table, and with all the maturity of a 40-year-old, I told them that if they weren't going to try, they could spend the rest of the day in their rooms. And off they went, crying and begging to continue with school.

I calmed myself down, and we tried it again, and the same exact thing happened. Isn't the definition of insanity doing the same thing again while expecting different results? I would have been labeled insane that day.

As I reflected on school that day, I tried to discern why I was so upset. It came down to I don't like halfhearted participation.

If you are going to do something, do it right. They weren't living up to their potential that day. They are smarter than that. They are better than that.

And so am I.

There's something to be said about the way we approach things in our life. While I firmly believe in always doing my best and giving it 100%, I don't live my life that way. I like to think I do, and I pride myself on the things that I am focused on because I am successful in those areas.

But truthfully, I'm not giving my all in everything.

- Folding clean clothes takes days to accomplish instead of 20 minutes.

- Putting away the folded clothes takes even longer.

- Patience is not on the top of my "giftings," and I don't take the effort to develop it further.

- I don't invest further into the relationships I am most secure in.

And those are just surface-level things. If I dig deeper, I would find a lot more with some grit.

I remember a song from my church camp days called "Casual Christian." While it was never a hit, we sang it around the campfire every year. The lyrics say:

> *I don't want to be a casual Christian.*
>
> *I don't want to live a lukewarm life.*
>
> *I want to light up the night*
>
> *With an everlasting light*

I don't want to live a casual Christian life.

Do I approach my relationship with Jesus with the same intentionality and vigor as other things in my life that are so important? Sometimes I do, and sometimes I don't. Some days living a sold-out, 100%-committed life to Jesus is harder than others. Some days I enjoy having a bad attitude. Some days I want to wallow in self-pity. Some days I just don't want to try as hard.

And on those days, I wonder if God might be hitting the table in frustration, saying, "You are better than this. Why aren't you trying harder?" But here's the catch, God knows everything I'm going to do before I do it. My sin doesn't surprise Him. He died for my sin. But my sins still make Him sad. He still wants me to grow to live in His righteousness more every day. I wonder if He's saying . . .

- Change the tone in your voice.

- Forgive that person.

- Stop exaggerating; it's a lie.

- Be more generous.

- Focus on Me, not them.

Why do we have trouble approaching the things most important to us with the vigor, energy, and vitality that defines them as the most important? So many reasons. But rather than finding excuses, let's just try harder.

Because God might be saying something similar that I said to my boys that day, something along the lines of "You are better than this! Just try!"

I apologized to my boys for how I acted and what I said that day. We still have moments when someone isn't doing their best. But now I can give more grace than before. I know that sometimes Revelation 3:16 is being directed at me: "But since you are like lukewarm water, neither hot nor cold, I will vomit you out of my mouth!" (*ESV*) Do I always give my best to God? Unfortunately, not. But I also know that when I do, I make Him proud. And when I don't, if I acknowledge that I'm not and try harder, I'm also making Him proud.

We don't expect our kids to be perfect, just to do their best. Don't you think God wants the same for us? Perfection isn't attainable; just do your best.

Chapter Ten: Hey Mom, I See You

Mother's Day is a special day. It's a day to celebrate the ladies in our life that we love so much. And being a mom myself, I get to be celebrated by the little people that I adore. But Mother's Day hasn't always been such a day of celebration.

Maybe your mom died recently, and this is another day with a poignant reminder that the person you love most isn't there to call. Or maybe you lost a child. And the person who should be celebrating you isn't here to do that—an unimaginable heartbreak.

After several years of marriage, my husband and I found out we were unable to have biological children. Mother's Day was already hard because of a longing in my heart. And now it was even harder. It was a reminder that I didn't have the one thing I wanted more than anything else. I imagine many others feel that same thing. It could be adoption, fertility treatments, or just a season of waiting. And in that waiting, there may be wondering and asking God, why me?

After years of infertility, we decided to adopt, but we had a failed adoption. We came home from the hospital to an empty nursery with empty arms and broken hearts. That season of struggling and questioning continued.

Wherever you are at, you are seen. You are seen by me, and you are seen by God. God knows about everything that we go through, and He cares, and He is there. Psalm 69:3 says, "I am worn out calling for help; my throat is parched. My eyes fail, looking for my God." (*NIV*)

So, mom, dad, I see you. This season you might feel like God is deaf to your cries or blind to your struggles. Or that He is just not going to answer your prayers. And you are left wondering. And you are left questioning. But I want you to know that God does see, and He does care. God can take all your heart, everything in this season of struggle in your life to redeem it. He will do something you can't even imagine.

When we were in the midst of our struggles, I clung to Joel 2:25, "The Lord will restore the years the locust hath eaten." (*KJV*) Being on the other side as a mom of four amazing little boys, I see the years that are restored. But I don't forget the season we were in. Wherever you are, I hope you know that God will take all your brokenness, all your pain, and all your questioning, and He will turn it around to do a redemptive work in your life. It might not be that you have a baby at the end of it because that's not what God promises. But God does promise to do something in you and through you.

When Jesus was in the garden of Gethsemane, he cried out to God, asking that the cup be taken from him, if at all possible. But God knew the only way to achieve his plan for humanity was for Jesus to go through that suffering. In the same way, God is going to use your suffering. He's not causing your suffering, but He will use it. And that is something I can wrap my arms around.

Chapter Eleven: Drift Happens

Before we had kids, we were perfect parents. We knew exactly how we would respond if our kids acted a certain way. And we knew they would always respond to our punishment positively with repentant hearts and changed behavior. Five years into this parenting gig, I know that we are far from perfect parents and our kids continue to disobey.

To be fair, most of the problem is my husband and me. Together we have agreed on behavior that is unacceptable in our family and what the punishment will be for specific actions. In our minds and through conversations when the kids are in bed, our plan seemed like it would work perfectly.

But then kids happen.

I see those big eyes look at me after they told a lie, and I don't want to punish them.

Taking away that privilege is going to put me out so much I let the behavior slide this time.

When I ask who did something, they willingly offer up themselves with a smile because they have no idea it will result in a punishment. (Gotta love the innocence of this one.)

It's the end of the day (or, let's be honest, morning), and I'm tired of refereeing and disciplining, so I don't.

Before I know it, I have drifted into lackadaisical parenting. We approached our parenting gig with guns blazing, ready to take on these four little lives we've been entrusted with. But life, and toddlers, wore us down.

Drift happens.

It's like when you are at the beach. You are out in the water enjoying the waves when you look back to shore and can't see your umbrella anywhere. Squinting down the beach, you see it far off in the distance and realize you've drifted and don't even know it.

My husband and I did not intend to lack follow-through in our parenting or discipline. But sometimes, it's as if we are in the middle of the ocean with diapers, meals, rowdiness, and just day-to-day life when we look back and see our standard way off in the distance. We must climb out of the chaos and work at getting back to where we started. To stay on track with our parenting, we need to always keep our eyes on what we laid out. And when the drift occurs, because it will, we need to refocus quickly rather than letting it continue to carry us away.

When one of my big guys was four, he told me that when he is a dad, he will let his kids do whatever they want so there won't be any crying or screaming. In his little mind, that makes sense, but I think that's when we start to let the drift happen.

I see it in my life. I know what I should do. I know what the standard is. But to avoid some screaming and crying, I don't do it. I drift into a pattern that wasn't my goal. Have you ever thought . . .?

- This month is tight, so I'm not going to tithe. But I'll do it next month. And next month doesn't come for a year.

- I'm really frustrated, so I raise my voice to make my point known. Tomorrow it's easier to raise my voice and maybe drop a word or two that isn't typically in my vocabulary. Before I know it, I have become bitter, and my words, spoken in anger, would make a sailor blush.

- I really like this guy I've been seeing. It's OK to do a little more. I still know where the boundary is. And without even realizing it, sex has become a part of your dates each week.

Without noticing, we have drifted away from what we know is right. We have drifted into a pattern of sin.

Drift happens. The only way to stop the drift from carrying you away is to acknowledge it. Know that it will happen, and do a daily/weekly/monthly check-in to see where you are. This takes some honesty. This takes humility. We don't like to admit that we are wrong. But we can never free ourselves from the drift without acknowledging that we are off course. Otherwise, you continue to drift further and further away from God.

Take charge of those patterns. Control them instead of letting them control you. It sounds a lot easier than it is. Depending on what your pattern is, you may need to find some professional help. At the very least, you need a good friend that will say the hard things and hold you accountable.

Satan loves the dark, and when we hide in the dark waters drifting along, he is winning. Don't let him win in your life. Take it back. Refocus on the truth. Get out of the water and run. Run to God, who is waiting for you. Every time you do that, you will find it a little easier. And pretty soon, you will feel the drift the moment it grabs your little toe.

Chapter Twelve: The Two Most Powerful Words

It's a moment I'll never forget. On Christmas morning, I was so excited for him to open his present. **I knew** he'd love it. I saved it for last. He watched his brother open a gift and was wiggling with excitement. Then it was his turn. There was a huge smile on his face as he ripped off the paper. Then his face fell.

No smile.

No excitement.

A look of disappointment that is forever embedded in my mind. He looked at me, then turned and walked away. He said nothing but in that look I saw. And my heart hurt.

I knew he would love that toy. **I knew** it was his favorite character. **I knew.**

I'm his mama. I love him. I know him. I understand him. And the gift that I picked out just for him was not what he wanted.

Six months later, I saw him playing with the toy he received for Christmas. He played with it all day. He carried it around the house. He wouldn't share it with his brothers. He loved it.

It took months for him to enjoy the gift he was given— months of sitting on a shelf collecting dust. Months of disappointment etched on my heart over a gift he didn't understand.

And then I read in Ephesians 2: 4, "**But God** . . ." *(NIV)* Two of the most powerful words in the Bible.

But God.

But God rich in mercy.

I love those words because they say that God is doing something amazing.

But how often do I whine and say, "But Go-ahd."

. . . why didn't I get what I asked for?

. . . why did this happen to me?

. . . where are you?

. . . why?

When we whine "but Go-ahd," we are diminishing God to a small 'g' god. He becomes a genie in a lamp that we think will give us whatever we ask for.

But GOD doesn't work that way. He gives us what He knows is best for us.

We have a big 'G' God.

But God.

But God . . . while we were still sinners.

But God . . . Christ died for us.

We think we know what we want, but God **knows** best. He **knows** our hearts. He **knows** what we need. He **knows** what we like to do. ***But God knows***.

We look to what other people have and long for that. We don't want what we have. But God **knows** best.

And months later, we will pick up that blessing and realize how great it is.

PART III: Spiritual Growth

Chapter Thirteen: A New Day

It was Thursday. I woke up just like every other Thursday leading up to this particular one. But as I lay in bed before the kids woke up, I knew today was different. Vastly different.

This Thursday was the first official day that I was a stay-at-home mom.

I had a barrage of emotions that I wasn't sure what to do with.

I was excited. Excited to spend more time with my kids and to train them up in the way of the Lord.

I was nervous. I knew it was going to be a huge adjustment, and I wasn't sure I was up to it.

I was sad. The day before ended an almost 17-year career I loved and poured so much into.

I was scared. I didn't know where God was taking my family on this journey, and I don't like not to know.

So . . . it was 9 AM, and the day was looming in front of me. I told myself that it was just like any other Thursday. But in my heart, I knew it was not the same. It was the beginning of unending days filled with whining, dirty diapers, a sink full of dishes, and breaking up fights.

That's if the glass is half empty. Which, in total transparency, is how I saw my life that morning.

Then I sat down with my Bible and a cup of coffee. I was reading Joshua 3 and God–He is so good. The Israelites were preparing to cross the Jordan River to reach the Promised Land. The river was wide, fast-flowing, and intimidating. The Levites were leading the nation of Israel and carrying the Ark of the Covenant. And this is what Joshua said:

"Do not come near it [the Ark], in order that you may know the way you shall go, for you have not passed this way before." (*ESV*)

Reading those words, I had tears streaming down my face. Don't get in front of the Ark, the presence of God, because you don't know where you are going–but He does. God is simply saying, 'Follow me. I know this is a new journey for you on a road you've never traveled. But don't worry. Follow me, and I will show you the way. I'll show you MY way.'

Oh, the tears of relief that God saw me exactly where I was and said, 'It's OK, I'm here.'

Then Joshua goes on to say, "Consecrate yourselves, for tomorrow the LORD will do wonders among you." (*ESV*, Joshua 3:5)

Oh, the wonders we will see when you lay aside all of us and focus on Him.

That morning I needed God to show up and sit with me. I needed Him to remind me that this new chapter in my life was His plan. I needed to take my eyes off the rushing water of being at home with four kids under the age of four. Instead, I needed to put my eyes on the presence of God.

When the Israelites were told to follow the Ark, it didn't change their circumstances. It changed their focus. And the change in focus changed their perspective.

When my eyes are on the presence of God, my circumstance will be the same: diapers, dishes, and whining kids. But my perspective will be different. I could see this as an opportunity that came from God to be more present and available to my family. It helped me to focus on what God is doing and going to do instead of on what I saw sitting right in front of me.

Joshua's faith was so strong. He lived out Joshua 1:8. "This Book of the Law shall not depart from your mouth, but you shall meditate on it day and night, so that you may be careful to do according to all that is written in it. For then, you will make your way prosperous, and then you will have good success. Have I not commanded you? Be strong and courageous. Do not be frightened, and do not be discouraged, for the Lord your God is with you wherever you go." (*ESV*)

This was a new journey for me. It came as a surprise. It came more quickly than I anticipated. But there I was. I shed a lot more tears in the coming days, but I rested in the assurance that if I focused on God and followed Him, I would see the LORD do wonders!

Chapter Fourteen: Control

There was a time when I was having some muscle pain in my shoulder and down my arm. Then my hand began to feel numb, and I had trouble holding things. It would come and go, but I had consistent discomfort for several weeks. Then I noticed something.

When I drive, I hold onto the steering wheel very tightly.

When I knit, I hold the needles very tightly.

When I write, I have a tight hold on the pen.

I realized I often have a tight hold on things in my life. Or, to put it more bluntly, I like to control things. And it seems this tight hold began to affect other areas of my life. When I hold tightly to something for too long, I begin to suffer physical pain.

Recognizing this need to hold tightly to the steering wheel when I'm driving allowed the Holy Spirit to open my heart to something even greater. (Something I've been struggling with but couldn't quite put into words.)

I hold too tightly to my children.

I like my little ducks to be with me all the time. I like to know they are safe, and if they are with me, I can keep them safe. Even when they get in the car to go off with my husband (who is an AMAZING father), I get nervous. I can't control them and protect them if they aren't with me.

I know this is not healthy. I know this is detrimental to my kid's development. I know it's not good for me. I know.

But it's hard. It's so hard.

In my healthy momming moments, I can recognize that I am holding on to them too tightly. And I can recognize that when my hold is that tight, I'm not really controlling them. They are controlling me.

I have chosen not to do things because I don't want to be away from my kids. They controlled me.

I have worried when they are away from me, so I don't enjoy the time alone. They controlled me.

I have said 'no' to them doing things or going places because they would be away from me. They controlled me.

It makes sense to hold tight to the things we love. But so much of our walk with God is going against what makes sense. When I hold tight to the things, I love I'm not letting God hold on. I'm trusting me over Him. I think I can take better care of my kids than He can.

One of my favorite verses from Psalms says, "Some trust in chariots and some in horses, but we trust in the name of the Lord our God" (*ESV*). Trust in God. Trust in His power and His goodness. Let go of the tight hold. Loosen the grip.

To hold loosely is to trust God more than myself.

- Trust He wants what is best.

- Trust He will protect them.

- Trust He knows what is best.

- Trust He will watch over them.

And to be honest, it scares me to let go, but it also scares me to hold on. So, I have stood in fear. If I let go, something can happen. If I hold on, God will force me to let go. You see, God doesn't care about my comfort. God cares about my heart. If my kids have become too much of a focus, God will address it.

Just like my shoulder and arm, when you hold too tightly to things for too long, you begin to suffer pain. If I continue to hold too tightly to my kids, I am confident that pain will come.

Physical pain. I will give up taking care of my body so I can always be with them. I won't join the gym, go on a bike ride or make that doctor's appointment.

Emotional pain. I will place my kids above time, allowing my mind to rest. I will allow their interests and needs to overtake my needs and my marriage.

Spiritual pain. I miss out on time spent just with God. I will pass up opportunities to go away on a retreat or a mission trip where God would be my focus.

It's easy to say trust God or have faith, but it's not as easy to put into practice. It's a choice I must make again and again. When we decide to drive two cars, and some of the kids go with my husband, I have to trust. When I am not home for dinner, I have to trust. When I go away overnight, I have to trust.

What I am learning is that I can hold onto my children— and I should—but not too tightly.

Because if I hold too tight, God will have to pry my fingers open, and that is never a good thing.

So, when you see me hovering or controlling my little people too much, please don't judge or offer advice. Because I know. Instead, just smile to yourself and say a prayer for me. I'm a work in progress. I may get it right today, but tomorrow may be a flop. Thankfully, God is patient, and He gently nudges me toward Him.

Chapter Fifteen: Good and Evil

I don't know when I first realized the battle of good and evil, but I know it's real. I just never thought I'd be helping my 3.5-year-old son realize there is a battle going on all around him.

We just spent a week at Disney, which is full of princesses and fairy tales. But every story has a villain. It didn't take him long to realize that every story has a dark side. Every ride we went on, every show we saw, every line we were in, he asked . . .

"Is there a bad guy?"

"Is he going to kill me?"

"Is he going to hurt me?"

"Where's the bad guy?"

And in every line, I said, "There's no bad guy. Mama won't let anything happen to you." But as I said those words, I knew deep in my heart I wasn't being honest. There is a bad guy. And as much as I want to protect my son, I know at some point he will get hurt.

So rather than telling him that the bad guys aren't real, I decided to let him know how real they are. There is a bad guy who is battling for a kingdom greater than the ones in fairy tales. He is more vicious than Scar, meaner than the wicked stepmother, and more powerful than any dragon. And he will fight to the bitter end.

But the good news is that in every story, good wins. Good will always prevail. Light will shine, and darkness will be dispelled.

So, I will tell my son that there are bad guys, but he doesn't need to be afraid. He has the greatest good on his side. A good that was powerful enough to rise from the dead and crush the bad guy once and for all.

Chapter Sixteen: Four Letter Words

The first time he said it, we were shocked! Where did he hear that? How does he even know that word?

So, we talked about it. We told him what it meant. We told him that we don't use that word in our family–ever. (Even though I may occasionally slip up.) We told him how that word hurts God's ears and heart. And we told him to never, ever say it again.

Weeks later, the movie he wanted to watch wasn't what was picked. So, he put his face in the couch and said, D@&m, d@&m, d@&m. My reaction was a mixture of shock (that he said it again) and amazement (that he used it correctly). He was punished and sternly reminded that we do not use that word in our house.

Two days later, he tripped over something and, without missing a beat, said, D@&m. And immediately, he looked at me with those big eyes and covered his mouth. He knew he was wrong, and he knew he had been caught.

In complete frustration, I asked him again where he had heard that word. And he finally gave me an honest answer. "It's on Ninja Turtles, mom. And I just want to be like them."

I felt like my mind was a slot machine at that point, and all the tiles clicked into place. Now I understood.

This little boy of mine loves anyone who takes down the bad guys. When you ask him what he wants to be when he grows up, his answer will always be some kind of superhero. So naturally, he would love the Ninja Turtles and want to be like them.

When his daddy got home from work, they had a long talk about how our family lives by a standard that not everyone else does. We can't do everything other people do or say everything other people say. Even if those people are really good or nice or cool (like the Ninja Turtles), we can't always act like them.

And for his punishment, he had to get out this movie that he loves and smash it to pieces with a hammer. And his heart was destroyed along with that DVD. He cried for hours over this loss.

It reminded me of how God commanded the Israelites to tear down the Asherah poles of every nation they conquered.

When the Israelites conquered a nation, they got rid of many practices of idolatry. But every time they left the Asherah poles up, they would fall back into disobedience. But if the poles were torn down, they chose to follow and obey God.

Just saying we will no longer live a certain way or do a certain thing isn't enough. We may know it is wrong like my little man knew that word was wrong, but we continue to sin. There is something cleansing and redeeming about removing from our lives the thing that is causing us to stumble.

Sometimes it's easy, like throwing out the Oreos when you are trying to lose weight. But it's not always as easy to take down your Facebook account because you are coveting your friend's life. It's not as easy to cut off your cable, so you aren't able to watch that show anymore. To delete contacts from your phone so you are no longer able to call that person.

Sometimes the temptation to live a life of sin is so strong, that the only way to overcome it is by surgically removing that temptation from your life. Take a hammer to it. Smash it to pieces. Get it out of your way.

The words are still in my son's head. And we are working with him on that. But giving him to power to overcome has been life-giving to him. And while I don't think this experience has totally wiped this word from his vocabulary, "Mom, I'm not going to say bad words anymore like stupid or d@&m," I think it taught him a great lesson.

"Finally brothers, whatever is true, whatever is noble, whatever is right, whatever is pure, whatever is lovely, whatever is admirable–if anything is excellent or praiseworthy–think about such things." (*NIV*)

Chapter Seventeen: A Thought on Thankfulness

With Halloween just a few days ago, I was reminded of our experience trick-or-treating with toddlers.

At the beginning of the night, they said, "trick or treat" and "thank you" without being prompted.

Halfway through, it was only "thank you."

When we called it quits, they were saying "give me candy," and we had to remind them to say "thank you," which was done while walking away.

In the beginning, when they didn't have much candy, they were excited and thankful. As their bags were filling up, they began to feel entitled and less appreciative of the gift of candy. It became less special as they received more and more.

How often do I feel entitled when I am blessed rather than being thankful for all I have been given? A little too often.

I want to focus on being thankful for what I have, instead of what I don't have, and to teach that to my children as well.

Chapter Eighteen: One Step

One of my kids was a really late walker. He preferred to scoot around on his bottom to get around. He was really good at it, so he didn't have much motivation to learn to walk. He's been walking for about ten months but is still hesitant. He's often unsure about his next steps. Even a tiny step off a sidewalk will have him sitting down and scooting to the road. He walks carefully and says, "hold your hand" when it's not a perfectly smooth surface.

I see myself in this. I like a smooth path - one without bumps or curves. A path that is straight, and you can see for miles down the road. But life isn't always a straight and smooth path.

When Saul met Jesus on the road to Damascus, it was like he hit the bumps of all bumps. It stopped him in his tracks and brought him to his knees. And in this position of forced humility, the instructions he received were, "Now get up and go into the city, and you will be told what you must do." (*NIV*, Acts 9:6) He was blind to the path in front of him (in every sense). He wasn't told what was next. He was just told to go, and then he would be told what was next. (And I love that Ananias was told to find Saul on Straight Street. I'd like to live on Straight Street right now.)

Like Saul, sometimes, we are only given one step at a time. We can't see the whole plan God has for us. But we just need to trust Him and take that step. Take the next step and let Him light up the one after that. Then take that step and wait for Him to show you the next.

It's slow.

It's frustrating.

It's scary.

It's faith-building.

I remember being in seasons of next steps when I questioned what was next. I wondered where we were going. I asked how it was going to work. I sought God to know what we should be doing. It was hard. It brought me to my knees. It brought me to tears. But with each step, God faithfully showed me another one. Not always in my time. But it was always there.

So, like my hesitant little boy, I'll scoot along the path. And daily, I will say, "hold Your hand." And like a loving parent, He will hold my hand. He will help me over the "huge and scary" bump. Because to God, it's not too big of a bump. It's a natural step in the road to get to where I'm going.

So I will walk.

And I will trust.

And I won't let go of His hand.

Chapter Nineteen: The Masks We Wear

In my house we love masks. Superhero masks. Robot masks. One even wears shorts/underwear on his head as a mask. Don't ask; I don't really understand it either.

When they put on a mask, they become someone else. It empowers them to take on characteristics they don't normally possess, like the ability to fly or the ability to fight all the bad guys. And my personal favorite, the ability to be invisible.

But what they don't understand quite yet is that even with their mask on, I can see the real them. It may hide their face or a piece of their face, but I still know who they are.

And in two and four-year-old rationale, they don't understand that. They don't get that wearing a mask doesn't change their capabilities. They still can't fly. They still only have the fighting powers of awkward four-year-olds. And they still aren't invisible.

They think things have changed.

It may be my fault. I play along. I pretend I can't see them. I pretend they have extra strength. I pretend they are someone else.

Or maybe it's my fault because I put on my own masks regularly.

I have it all together.

I always look like I do on Sunday at church.

My life is exactly what it looks like on social media.

My house is always clean and laundry is always done.

I have so many friends, and I am so busy having fun with them.

I want my life to be a certain way, so I put on a mask and pretend to be someone I'm not. And if I wear my mask long enough, it starts to become a part of me. Maybe not the real me, but a part of my perception of me.

Can I just say, "LET'S TAKE OFF THE MASKS!"

Take them off. Step on them. Throw them away. Let's stop pretending to be someone we aren't. Let's stop trying to be someone we aren't. Let's be who God made us to be. Not who we want to be. Not who other people think we should be. Let's be the real us.

When we put on masks, it's like we are saying we aren't good enough. We think we need to be better. We think we don't measure up. These are lies straight from the pits of hell. Throw away the lies. Crush them under your heel. Let the truth set you free.

Ephesians 2:10 "For we are his workmanship, created in Christ Jesus for good works, which God prepared beforehand, that we should walk in them." (*ESV*)

Psalm 139:14 "I praise you for I am fearfully and wonderfully made." (*ESV*)

Romans 8:37 ". . . we are more than conquerors through him who loved us." (*ESV*)

When our masks are off, we can live in freedom. We can live as we were intended to live. So, take off the mask. Be real. Be who you are. Be honest. (A word of advice: be honest within reason. Social media isn't the place to bear it all. Find a trusted friend to confide in.) The point is, let's stop pretending we have it all together.

I'll be the first to say I don't have it all together, even if it looks like that sometimes. You missed dinner the night my husband asked if I was going to "look like that all the time now that I'm staying at home" or would I sometimes, you know, do my hair?

I looked nice when I showed up at church on Sunday? I squeezed into the dress, and that morning was probably the first shower I had taken in three days. And to pull off the easy look, I had to get up at 5 AM. Were my kids dressed too? That most likely means there was some whining and yelling involved.

When I post pictures on social media, I choose ones that make me smile and help me remember a moment. And honestly, I don't want to remember all the temper tantrums that happened that day. But don't judge my life and my kids by what you see. At any given moment, someone has just been disciplined or is just about to be disciplined.

Does my house always look clean in pictures? You too can angle a shot to block out the pile of laundry or sink full of dishes! And honestly, my husband cleans the house regularly—like he vacuums almost every night. I can count on one hand the times I've done dishes since we were married. And this week, my kids have been taking shorts out of the dirty clothes for two days because laundry needs to be done.

Do you think we are so busy with friends? Guess what? I get lonely too. There are days that go by, and I've only talked to the people that live in my house. I long for adult conversation. I envy the fun things you do with all your friends.

Can we all be real? Can we stop pretending? Can we lay down our masks?

Can we celebrate the bad hair days along with the heels? Can we celebrate laundry that is folded along with toys that are scattered all over the house? Can we join one another and be who we are?

Let's do it together.

For ourselves. For our friends. For strangers at the grocery store. For our kids. For God.

Because being us is so much better than being something else.

Chapter Twenty: We're Home

We are at church a lot. While I worked there, it was a whole lot. Every time we pulled into the parking lot, one of my littles would say, "We're home!"

Cute, right? But when I thought about it, we should feel at home when we're at church.

Home is a place where we belong.

Home is where a family meets backs up.

Home is a place where we are comfortable, where we can kick off our shoes and be us.

Home is a place to rest and recharge.

And isn't that what the church should be?

At church, we find belonging. We find ourselves surrounded by people who have the same values. While we all have our own opinions, just like a family, we can still agree on core values that help define who we are.

Church is where every week, or maybe more often, we can meet back up and connect with others. We've been out all week, but when we are together, we can talk, encourage one another, and laugh together.

When we are at church, we should be able to be our true selves, not who we think we should be, not who we are told we should be. When we come to church, we come as we are: as sinners and broken people. Regardless of the level of brokenness, we are still loved and accepted.

At church we can find rest for our soul. It's a time when we are refilled with the Spirit of God.

Church is a lot like home, but home isn't always quiet and peaceful.

Think about when a new baby comes into a family. It gets sloppy—at least it did in my family. We had to change our schedule, our expectations, our routine. We moved chairs around at the dinner table to make room for high chairs. We had to learn about these new family members, which took time. But the work was worth it because we loved these new members of our family as much as we loved the ones who had been there for years.

So, what is your church like? Is it a family that welcomes everyone home?

Think about it.

At church, do we love and welcome every new person? We may say we do, but what about when you must rearrange where you sit to make room? What about when you have to get there earlier because you are parking farther away to allow a new family to have the best parking spot? How about talking to new people and including them in your conversations? Do we welcome everyone in even when it's hard? I'm not always sure.

I want my attitude toward the church to be like my sons, "I'm home!"

If you come every week, I want you to feel at home.

If it's your first time, I want you to feel at home.

If you left years ago and are coming back, I want you to feel at home.

If you are broken and lost, I want you to feel at home.

If you are a different color, race, or income level; if you have 50 tattoos or none at all; if you have on a dress or shorts; no matter who you are or what you look like, I want you to feel at home.

Because here's the deal: the church is just an example of what heaven will be like. And when we run home with our arms open wide and smiles on our faces, we will be welcomed. We will find rest. We will find family. We will find love and acceptance.

So run. Run hard. Run fast. Run home.

And when my little says, "We're home!" my response is, "Yes baby, we are home."

Chapter Twenty-One: Let Me Eat

Every morning when I got the babies up, the first thing they asked was, "Where's daddy?"

The next thing they said was, "What's for dinner?" I'm not sure if they are asking what is for dinner or if they aren't using breakfast, lunch, and dinner appropriately—either way, they want to know what they are eating that day.

They love to eat. While eating one meal, the big boys are asking what's for the next. This may be a habit picked up from me. I love to eat and look forward to my next meal while finishing the current one.

And don't even think of asking my husband to miss a meal. He likes his three meals every day. He doesn't like to skip one and eat a bigger meal later. Nope. He wants to eat the right way (which means three meals).

Jesus said I am the bread of life (*NIV*, John 6:36). He is our sustenance. He gives us our nutrition. In the Lord's Prayer, we are taught to pray, "Give us this day our daily bread" (*NIV*, Matthew 6:11). We do want to ask God for our literal food, but I wonder, shouldn't we also be asking Him to give us a portion of Jesus every day?

Just like we need to eat real food regularly and consistently, we need to be with Jesus, partaking of the bread of life, regularly.

If we miss too many meals, we become weak and sick. It affects our mood, our health, our focus, and so much more.

When we miss time with Jesus, it affects us. We become spiritually weak. We lose our focus. We become selfish, moody, lifeless.

Let's all live the way my kids do, saying, "What am I going to eat next?" Let's look forward to the next meal with Jesus, to the next time we sit with Him.

Feast on the bread of life.

Chapter Twenty-Two: What Do You Want?

Every Saturday morning, I ask the boys what they want for dinner the next week. One of them will always make a request or two. And the next week for dinner we are eating what he requested. This week I started to think the other big boy doesn't ever get something he loves for dinner. But then I realized he never asks for anything.

Sure, I'll get him chicken nuggets or cherries or another one of his favorite things to eat. But I never made something for dinner because he requested it. Sometimes I feel bad about it . . . for about two minutes. But then my pragmatic side kicks in, and I think, "if he doesn't ask, then I can't give it to him."

Two seconds after that, the Holy Spirit starts nudging me. James 4:2 says, ". . . You do not have because you do not ask." (*ESV*)

Wow! It makes me reevaluate how I pray—what I talk to God about.

Do I truly layout my desires before God? Or do I just wait for Him to give me things? Am I missing out on some amazing things because I don't ask—because I assume He knows what I need and want? I feel like that answer is a resounding YES!

Does my guy just assume I know what he likes to eat, so he trusts me to provide? I'm sure he does. But he's also missing out on some amazing things, some of his favorites, because he doesn't ask.

I WANT to give my guys amazing things, and I'm positive God wants to give me amazing things too. But sometimes I think He's just waiting for me to say, "Hey Dad, can I have something special?"

Chapter Twenty-Three: Guilt vs. Repentance

One of my boys says, "I'm sorry" all the time.

He falls down. "I'm sorry."

He throws up. "I'm sorry."

He trips. "I'm sorry."

He mispronounces a word. "I'm sorry."

I imagine he apologizes about ten times a day. It's usually over something silly or something that was a complete accident and sometimes, over something that wasn't even wrong.

But there are other times when he does do something wrong.

He hits his brother.

He calls someone a name.

He tells me no.

He disobeys.

These are the moments when he doesn't say "I'm sorry" without some parental guidance.

Why does he apologize for simple things that require no apology but digs in his heels when he needs to apologize?

I think the difference is guilt versus repentance.

Guilt is a feeling that you deserve blame or punishment. Guilt is from Satan.

Repentance is having sincere regret over your actions. Repentance is from God.

When it's something simple, he feels like he is to blame for what just happened. He threw up and thinks he is to blame for the mess that needs to be cleaned up. He tripped over my foot and thinks he is to blame that I may be hurt.

Guilt is a feeling that Satan sets in our mind. A feeling of inadequacy. A feeling that we are wrong. A feeling that we didn't do it right.

On the other hand, repentance is acknowledging your actions and showing sincere regret over them. Sincere enough that you will change how you act and live.

When he truly does something wrong, he realizes he was wrong but not enough to change his behavior. He digs in his feet. He won't apologize. He makes excuses for his behavior.

I'm always amazed at how my actions are so similar to my three-year-olds.

- I feel guilty about things I do.

- I should have spent more time playing with my kids.

- I wish I had saved that money instead of buying a new pair of shoes.

- I should have eaten the apple instead of the cookie.

But repentance? That's hard.

- Do I repentant when I lose my temper?

- Do I regret my actions when I lash out in anger over a situation?

- Do I repent when I talk about someone unkindly or behind their back?

We need to move past feeling guilty for simple things that keep us in bondage. Instead, we need to repent of the things that keep us from God. If we choose to block out the lies of Satan, we are choosing to live in freedom. If we choose to repent and turn from our sin in our lives, we are choosing to walk with Christ. And walking with Christ makes our lives so much fuller.

So, as I'm teaching my son to live a life of spiritual freedom, I will be reminding myself of the same thing.

Chapter Twenty-Four: Dressed to Impress

One of my big boys loves for people to notice him. And not just notice him but compliment him. He has a deep desire to be liked by everyone. He will dress in a tie because someone told him that he looked sharp. He will say a certain thing because someone commented how funny or smart he was. He will act a certain way to get a positive response from those important to him. One day he whispered all day because he heard me tell a friend they were quiet that day. He wanted to be noticed and acknowledged, even though he had no idea what that really meant.

I love this little boy of mine so deeply. I love everything about him. What he doesn't understand yet is that my love for him isn't based on what he does or does not do. It's because I am his mom, and I have a deep, unconditional love for every piece of him.

When I see him trying to find love in this earthly world, my heart is sad. I tell him his value is not in what he does or how he looks. I explain that his value comes through who he is. And I praise him for who he is. I tire my brain out coming up with new adjectives to explain what an amazing, kind, sensitive, funny, smart little boy he is.

Now I am not the mom to encourage my kids to pump up their self-esteem, read ego. I think we can all do that just fine on our own. What I am attempting to show him is that our value is not from ourselves or others. Our value in this world is pennies. But in the spiritual, eternal world, his value is worth far more than anything we can express.

As I tell my sweet boy that how he dresses or looks isn't important, I worry about my own life, how the scale keeps moving in the wrong direction. I worry that my jeans are out of style. I

71

spend too much time looking at shoes that my bank account can't purchase. I wear lipstick, curl my hair, and don't eat sugar in order to look and feel a certain way. And then I compare myself to you. I see how beautiful your hair looks and buy the same products. I envy your size 6 jeans and go home to binge on carbs.

While I know deep in my soul that my worth doesn't come from any of this stuff, I still chase it. That's not to say we can't desire to look nice, have nice clothes or be healthy. It's when those things, the desire to be someone else with those things, outweighs who are that it is a problem.

I am not a woman who wants to be three sizes smaller.

I am not a woman who envies those with the biggest closet or trend-setting clothes.

I am not a woman who needs to wear lipstick to be put together.

I am more than that. I am a woman who is deeply loved by God. I am a woman who longs to know God intimately. I am a woman who walks with God, who trips in that walk daily, but who continually rises. God doesn't care about my waist or what babies have done to my body. God cares about my heart. Is my heart pure? Repentant? Generous? Kind? That's what truly matters.

I know that I am passing on some bad habits to my kids. Maybe my guy's desire to impress with his outward appearance and actions came from me. I'm sure some of it did unknowingly. But I also hope that he will learn that true love and acceptance from Jesus is where I will hang my hat.

Chapter Twenty-Five: Dirt

Ugh—little boys are dirty. And they stink. Every day I make my kids play outside for at least one hour. Mine seem to think that the raised gardens were placed there just for them to dig in. They find a stick—from where I have no idea, it seems little boys are able to create these out of nothing—and use it to fling dirt out of the garden and into the face of their brother. Many days when I call them in for lunch, someone's hair is filled with dirt and grit. The level of uncleanliness they can bear baffles me. Mainly because if they get a drop of spaghetti sauce on their shirt at dinner, it becomes as important as global warming.

On especially dirty days, they strip down to their birthday suits at the back door and take the walk of shame straight to the bathroom. I turn on the shower, and while listening to the screams of four little boys reverberate off the bathroom tiles, I do my best to get them clean as quickly as possible.

It's a fairly traumatic experience for all of us.

Getting dirty is a natural part of life. And getting clean is a natural response to the dirt.

I think of those who were unclean throughout the Bible—lepers or those who came in contact with dead bodies. Because of their uncleanliness, they were forced to live outside the camp.

Years ago, I visited a leper colony in west Africa. It was such a sad place to visit. These people were forced to live away from everyone and everything because of their disease. They were cut off and shunned from society. It was no fault of their own, just fate, destiny, bad luck—call it what you want.

While we can see the sadness of this situation, I can see the irony of it as well. We have all, at times, found ourselves symbolically unclean and living outside the camp. When we have unconfessed sin in our lives, it separates us from God. It's only through the blood of Jesus that we can enter into the presence of God.

In the camp, where God dwells, we find relationships, security, value . . . But what of those who are not there? They are living with isolation and darkness that comes from the light of Jesus not shining on them.

Don't we want everyone to come into the light? To come into that perfect restorative relationship with Jesus. 1 John tells us, "But if we walk in the light, as he is in the light, we have fellowship with one another, and the blood of Jesus his Son purifies us from all sin." (*ESV*, 1 John 1:7) When I visited the leper colony, it broke my heart to see so many people living in such pain. Do I feel the same way when I see people living in the darkness of the Gospel? Do I long for them to find healing and an open-armed welcome into the community of believers?

When I see my kids filthy from being outside, my natural reaction is to clean them off so they can come into the house. When we see people living outside of the camp, outside of having a life-changing relationship with Jesus, shouldn't our same reaction be to help them find cleansing?

So, what are we doing? What am I doing? Honestly, not enough. Eternity is at stake, but sometimes I view it just as life choices that don't align with mine. I can disagree with their choices, or lack thereof, but not enough to talk about their choices with them.

I would never dream of letting my kids walk through life covered in dirt. Yet there are people in my life, people that I love to my core, who are walking around covered in the dirt of sin that can only be removed by the blood of Jesus. I'm not going to talk to them about how dirty they are. That accomplishes nothing. But I will welcome them into my life and home, dirt and all. And I will pray they will see the difference in me and choose to accept the redemptive cleansing of Jesus. It may take 1,000 cups of coffee to get there, but in the end, it will be worth it all. So, I'm getting out my coffee pot and praying that God will continue to use me to draw more people to Him.

Chapter Twenty-Six: What's in a Name

My kids are at ages where names are important. My big boys want to know everyone's full name. Not just mom or Gammy or Pap, but real names. And my little boys are into name-calling. Mr. Poopypants and Grumpyface are the top two names I hear being called out.

A name.

It's important.

When we were pregnant, I remember the struggle of coming up with names. My second pregnancy was especially hard; we were having our third and fourth boys within 18 months of each other and were tapped out on boy names. It felt like a lot of pressure to choose a name. It had to flow. It had to 'go with' our last name. It had to be a name that we would like for the rest of our lives.

A name.

It carries a lot.

There were names my husband liked but reminded me of someone I once knew who was annoying or mean or just rubbed me the wrong way. Or my husband would pick a name just because they were a great baseball player. But now that we have named our boys, and they have lived with those names for several years, I can't imagine them being anyone else. All the other names we thought of just don't fit. Is it because we chose the correct name or because they grew into the name we chose?

A name.

It defines us.

In the Gospels, Jesus once asked his disciples, "Who do you say I am?" (*NIV*, Matthew 16:15) A simple question. But is it really? Who is Jesus? And the real question, who is Jesus *to you?* Jesus was called by lots of names throughout the Bible. People were confused about who He was. People didn't understand what His name actually meant.

But none of that confusion changed who He is. He is still Messiah. He is still the Son of God. He still *is.*

PART IV: Trending

Chapter Twenty-Seven: Call It by Name

I'm scared. I know what I want to say, but I'm scared. I've shared pieces of this story over the years. I've even shared the whole story with some groups. But they were groups of strangers.

But knowing that friends will read this–people I love–that makes it even harder. I want to appear strong. I want to appear like I don't struggle. But that's just me protecting myself with a mask.

So, in total transparency, I'm taking off this mask and showing you the truth of what lies underneath. And I hope in the end this can help someone else and glorify God. (I'm not looking for pats on the back with this. I'm truly hoping my story will encourage someone else.)

This story took place in 2007. In February of that year, my world went dark. I felt like everything just fell apart around me. It felt like everything in my life, everything that was important to me was lost. That was a lie of Satan, but can't we all agree it's really easy to believe him over God sometimes. And when I started to believe those lies, I began falling into a pit that Satan had made just for me.

It started with simple isolation. I cut myself off from friends and family. I was crying all the time, and when I looked at my life, it all seemed hopeless. Every day it got worse. I was sleeping 12-14 hours a day and was still tired. I stopped eating. I stepped away from all the relationships in my life. Finally, a good friend told me I needed to call the doctor. I did and was diagnosed with clinical depression.

I hated that label. It was harsh. It was humiliating. It was scary.

Would people think I was weak? Would people whisper that I just needed to "suck it up" and keep going with life? Would people still like me?

I quickly forgot about those fears because my depression was sucking me in deeper and deeper. I couldn't concentrate. I couldn't make any decisions. I cried all the time. I felt . . .

   . . . inadequate

   . . . lonely

   . . . lost

   . . . hopeless

   . . . alone.

I stopped wanting to be around other people. If I spent too much time with others, I became mean and started to make inappropriate comments. I was like a three-year-old child that spoke their mind and needed constant adult supervision.

My phone would ring all day. Sometimes it was friends who knew what I was going through and called to check on me. Other times it was just people in my life calling to talk. Regardless of who it was, I didn't answer the phone. I didn't listen to my voicemail or call anyone back. This was before text messaging was the preferred form of communication, but I would have ignored those as well. I was shutting myself away more and more.

Not only that, but I couldn't manage to do normal, everyday things. I had to follow a schedule a friend had made me:

     10:30: wake up

     10:40: walk the dog

     11:00: make coffee and eat breakfast

11:30: brush teeth

12:00: work out

1:00: time with God

2:30: take a shower

When I look at this list now, I see how dire the situation was. If I didn't look at the refrigerator to know what to do next, these things wouldn't have gotten done. I can't tell you the number of days I did nothing but stay in bed all day. But even the schedule had its problems. If I completed a task early, I would get back in bed or sit on the couch and stare until it was time to do the next thing. I was completely incapable of making my own decisions and choices.

My counselor described depression this way: he said, you see a cup on the counter, and you know that you should put the cup away, but you don't know how to put the cup away, and you really don't want to put the cup away, but you know you should put the cup away, but you're just not sure you can put the cup away. Before you know it, you've spent 30 minutes obsessing over what to do with the cup, and you end up leaving it on the counter and going back to bed.

For me, depression seemed like being underwater. You can see and hear everything that's going on around you, but it's all messed up. You can see the light and hear the laughter, and you want to join in, but you're incapable. And nothing you can do can get you out of the water to participate in life again. You just can't will yourself out of it.

Some well-intentioned people said I just needed to pray more. I just needed to spend more time with God. I tried and got mad when God didn't answer. For months He didn't answer. He didn't say anything—or I wasn't really listening. It got to a point where I didn't want to pray; I didn't want to talk to God or about God or even crack my Bible. I had no desire to engage in any activity that God was a part of, even if it was my life.

I only heard God say one thing to me at all at the very beginning. He reminded me of the story in Daniel when Daniel prayed to God for deliverance, and it took 21 days for an angel to show up. When he finally did, Daniel asked why God didn't answer immediately. The angel said God immediately heard and responded to Daniel's prayer, but the angel was so busy fighting in the spiritual world that it took him this long to get there. God assured me that things might get bad, but He is there fighting a battle for me that I couldn't see. He was winning a war but would come and deliver me as soon as He could. That continued to give me hope even on the darkest days that I wasn't alone, and this depression wouldn't destroy me.

My darkest days were when I was on a cruise with friends. It should have been a great trip, but I didn't have my refrigerator schedule to look at anymore. I had to rely on my friends to take care of me. I was glad to be out of Savannah and away from some very destructive temptations, but the rebellion was still there. One afternoon there was no plan. I tried so hard to be an adult and take care of myself, but I couldn't. I tried sleeping, but it wouldn't come. I tried reading but was bored and unfocused. I tried walking around the ship watching the waves but was uninterested. I found myself on the top deck of the ship staring out to sea. Then I thought of jumping off the boat.

Here were my thoughts: "I could jump off that side of the boat onto the dock where it's cement. But will it really kill me or just break a lot of bones, and I'll be worse off than I am now. I could jump off this side of the boat into the water, but what will really happen to me. It's too bad we're not moving so I could be left out at sea alone. Or I could go sit at the bar and get completely drunk." None of those were good options, and thankfully I realized that.

I could go on and on with stories of how hard things were. I tried to spend time with God. I was starting to hear His voice again, thanks to the many people that were praying for me. But I didn't feel l like I was getting any better. I was on medication, but I didn't feel like it kicked in. I was in counseling, but I didn't like that either. Nothing satisfied me.

Then, all of a sudden (to me but not to the many people who were praying so hard for me), I woke up one day and felt like a light switch had been flipped in me. I was alive. I didn't have to look at my schedule to know what to do. I started answering my phone more often, although not all the time. I would talk to more people and leave the house more often. The change was amazing. I started journaling more and reading the Bible again. Before that, all I could do was go over note cards of Bible verses I was memorizing. But again, God's Word is eternal. There were so many verses that got me through this like:

Isaiah 43:10 "' You are my witnesses,' declares the Lord, 'and my servant whom I have chosen, that you may know and believe me and understand that I am he. Before me no god was formed, nor will there be any after me.'" (*ESV*)

Deuteronomy 31:6 "Be strong and courageous. Do not be afraid or terrified because of them, for the LORD your God goes with you; he will never leave you nor forsake you." (*NIV*)

Jeremiah 31:3 "I have loved you with an everlasting love." (*NIV*)

Philippians 4:19 "And my God will supply every need of yours according to His riches in glory in Christ Jesus." (*ESV*)

Psalm 40:1-3 "I waited patiently for the Lord; and He inclined to me and heard my cry. He brought me up out of the pit of destruction, out of the miry clay, and He set my feet upon a rock making my footsteps firm. He put a new song in my mouth, a song of praise to our God; many will see and fear and will trust in the Lord." (*NASV*)

James 4:8 "Draw near to God and He will draw near to you." (*NASV*)

Psalm 102:17 "He will respond to the prayer of the destitute. He will not despise their plea." (*NIV*)

Romans 8:28 "And we know that God causes all things to work together for good to those who love God, to those who are called according to His purpose." (*NASV*)

Philippians 1:6 "For I am confident of this very thing, that He who began a good work in you will perfect it until the day of Christ Jesus." (*NASV*)

The whole 27th Psalm but some verses in particular; verse 4 says, "One thing I have asked from the Lord, that I shall seek: that I may dwell in the house of the Lord all the days of my life." (NASB, 1995) And verse 8 says, "When You said, 'Seek My face,' my heart said to You, 'Your face O Lord, I shall seek.'" (*NASV*)

Isaiah 55:8-9 "For My thoughts are not your thoughts nor are your ways My ways. For as the heavens are higher than the earth so are My ways higher than your ways and my thoughts than your thoughts." (*NASV*)

This was the turning point for me. Every day I got better. Every day I talked to another person. Every day I got up and took a shower of my own initiative and trusted God as best I could. I continued with counseling and with prayer counseling. Both were very effective in pushing me past my own limits. Both allowed God to carry me from rock to rock as I climbed up out of the pit.

In the middle of my depression, I knew God would be teaching me something, but I didn't care. I knew I would come out refined and purified, but I didn't care. I didn't even care if I got out. I know that things were very bad in my life, but I don't think I'll ever truly know how bad it was. Those closest to me may have a better understanding of it than I do. But I do know God is faithful. God never left me alone; He never let go. When I wanted to jump off the ship or out of the parking garage, God was there pulling me backwards. When I wanted to sleep and never eat again, God put persistent people in my life to make sure I didn't waste away. A friend gave me two pieces of advice through this, and I hated both of them until I understood what she was talking about.

First, she said that I needed to fight it. What am I supposed to fight? I don't want to fight. I don't care about fighting, even if I knew what I was fighting. But then I realized what she meant one day when I chose to stay in bed. I didn't fight the depression. I didn't fight myself to get up, make my bed, eat and get a shower. If I had done that and left the house, I would have had a good day. But instead, I let Satan have that day and didn't fight. I gave up. I got it that day and determined that I would fight from then on.

She also told me that I needed to embrace the process. I honestly can't tell you how many times I heard that, but she knew what she was talking about. God was taking me through a process. God was refining me in the fire of life. And when gold is refined, it gets out all the impurities. And when the impurities are gone, the Goldsmith can see His reflection in the gold. I was in that fire, and I pray that God can see His reflection in me. He told me to glorify Him in the midst of my depression and afterwards. I pray that I continue to embrace the process that He has me on that I may truly glorify Him.

I wore my mask for too long. Instead of letting others see me for who I was, I hid. I even hid from myself. This is not what God wants for us. He doesn't want us to live a life of bondage, of hiding away. He has so much more for us.

I don't know where you are or what you've gone through. My hope is that we can all commit to some things together:

Bearing one another's burdens with love. If you know someone who is struggling with depression, walk alongside them in love.

Allowing the truth to set us free. Let's talk about it. Let's stop hiding behind our masks of shame and fear. If we talk about depression (and suicide), we can help normalize it, and maybe, in doing that, someone will ask for help before it's too late.

Seeking God with your whole heart. If you are in the midst of depression, seek God the best you can. Allow others into your life. Ask for help. Ask for prayer. It's hard, so hard, but it will make all the difference.

Depression is hard. It's scary. It was only when I allowed myself to be weak that I found my strength in God. And today, I can truly say, "You have turned my mourning into dancing; you have loosed my sackcloth and girded me with gladness, that my soul may sing praise to You and not be silent. O Lord my God, I will give thanks to You forever." (*NASV* Psalm 30:11-12)

Chapter Twenty-Eight: On the Other Side

From the time I graduated from college, I had a career in full-time ministry. I loved what I did. It was fun. It was challenging. And I knew that I was called to the ministry.

I was able to be a part of some amazing things while serving on staff at my church. I saw hundreds of kids accept Christ. I saw thousands of families grow stronger. I saw lives, families, and generations change because of Jesus.

They were some of the most fulfilling years of my life.

This summer Reid and I decided the next season of our family would mean me staying at home with our four boys. It has been a big, God-directed transition. One of the most surprising differences I have noticed is a change in me. I'm more patient. I'm more joyful. I'm more at peace.

While I'm excited about this change, in a way, it makes me very sad. I'm sad that only after I left full-time ministry that my outward expressions toward life changed.

Some of it is because I'm no longer doing two jobs. I'm now "just" a wife/mom. My energy, focus, and time aren't split between work and home.

The other part of the change is what bothers me. I think I am changed because life is so much easier when I'm not in ministry. Ministry is hard. There are countless people watching everything you do. And many of them freely offer advice, feedback, and criticism. You can't please everyone, but in the ministry, you try. Not because you are a people-pleaser but because you are a representation of Christ, and everything you do is to draw them closer to Jesus.

When you are in ministry, your life is a fishbowl. People watch how you dress, talk, act, treat your spouse, raise your kids . . . the list goes on and on. No matter where you go or what you do, you are on display.

The only place you can truly be yourself is in your home. But you aren't at your home too often. Evening services, volunteer meetings, church events, or phone calls with hurting church members take up a lot of the precious time you have at home.

Please know I am not saying any of this to complain or cast blame. I worked at an amazing church. The leadership was wonderful. The volunteers were the best. The members were kind and giving.

I am saying this because our church leaders should experience this joy and peace while they are serving in ministry.

And it's up to us to help them.

Let's make a commitment to support our leaders. We won't like everything our church leaders do. We may not like every sermon they preach or every song that is chosen. But can we take advice from Flower, "If you can't say anything nice, then don't say anything at all." Or perhaps advice from Paul, ". . . whatever is true, whatever is noble, whatever is right, whatever is pure, whatever is lovely, whatever is admirable—if anything is excellent or praiseworthy—think about [dare I interject, talk about] such things." (*NIV*, Philippians 4:8)

Church leaders need our encouragement more than our criticism. They need our support more than our complaints. They need our love more than our hate.

If something happens and you don't like it, spend some time praying before complaining. Many times, if not most, the

Holy Spirit will resolve the issue for us—in our heart as well as in our church.

Let's also commit to praying for our leaders. They need our prayers. They covet them. It's not just lip service. Their jobs literally depend on your prayers.

Pray for them to have times of rest and for that rest to be rejuvenating. Pray for them to follow God no matter what the cost. Pray for them to stay strong in their faith. Pray for them to be guarded against temptation. Pray for them to be protected from Satan. They need our prayers.

Working in a church is hard. It's lonely. But it's worth it.

In Joshua 17, we read of when Joshua and the Israelite's were fighting the Amalekites, and the battle was tense. When Moses held his staff above his head, Israel was strong. But when he lowered his arms, Israel began to be defeated. Moses could only support Israel for so long before he grew tired. Israel would have been defeated if it wasn't for Aaron and Hur. They came alongside Moses and gave him a stone to sit on. Then, they held up his arms when he could no longer do it himself.

Without the support of Aaron and Hur, Israel would have lost the battle. Without your support, what will happen to your church? Aaron and Hur didn't offer advice. They didn't criticize. They didn't tell Moses how to stand or how to hold his arms. They walked over to him and held up his arms.

Amazing things are happening in the church—in your church. What else could happen when we hold up our leaders? Your role in the church is just as important as theirs. God's Kingdom will grow when we work together. Together lives will be changed. Together we will change eternity.

Chapter Twenty-Nine: Taken

My kids love to read the Bible. And being a former Children's Pastor, we have plenty of Bible's for them to choose from. One of their favorites is a Bible that is illustrated in graphic novel style, and I totally understand why my four-year-old loves it.

Last week he brought that Bible to me and was asking questions about the pictures he saw. I looked down and saw he was in the book of Revelation. (No wonder he didn't know what he was really looking at. We don't typically read from Revelation at bedtime.) He loved the dragon and was amazed when I told him about the battle between God and Satan.

The next day I overheard this same four-year-old tell his brother, "Let's play. I'll be Satan."

After I was done choking on my coffee, I called him over and explained that he couldn't play Satan. "Can I be the dragon mom?" No, not the dragon either. Then I said, "we don't play Satan in our home." More words I never thought I would say before becoming a parent.

I've chuckled over this conversation numerous times since it happened. But the truth is, while we don't play Satan in our home, many people do play that game. Many people do assume that role. And that is scary.

I'm not talking about witchcraft or Ouija boards. I'm talking about people in our society that enslave the helpless. Did you know there are millions of people (think 20+ million, conservatively) enslaved in the sex trade around the world? This includes human trafficking (children as well as adults) and the sex industry (prostitution, strip clubs, etc.).

This makes me sad, angry, scared, horrified, disgusted . . . the adjectives could go on and on. I think about my precious little boys—innocent, kind, sensitive. I think about how I would feel if they were taken from me—ripped from my home—lured into slavery. Physically and emotionally tortured. And I have to stop there because I can't handle the thought of my child, any child, being hurt like that.

I think about little boys who should be asking Santa for bikes and Hot Wheels but instead are being sexually exploited. I think about little girls who should be making gingerbread cookies and dreaming of Barbie houses but are being defiled by disgusting men. I think of women who undress for a dollar because they are stuck in a situation they never dreamed they would be in with no apparent way out.

This is not what they dreamed Christmas would be like for them. This is not what Christmas *should* be like for them.

It breaks my heart and brings me to tears.

I'm reminded of the movie "Taken." The way Liam Neeson's character goes after every one to bring back his daughter shows how far someone will go for love. When he says, "I will look for you, I will find you, and I will kill you," we all want to stand up and cheer. He's the guy we would call if anything happened to someone we love.

Liam Neeson plays a fictional character. But there are people in our communities who are approaching this industry with the same vengeance his character did. There are men and women who are going into the thick of the battle every day just to bring one person home.

I'm going to be honest. For years I've prayed for a local ministry that is making a difference. But God is really stirring my heart right now. I don't know why. I don't know what. I don't know how. But I do know that that Satan is prowling around like a roaring lion seeking someone to devour (1 Peter 5:8). And we can't let him do that! There are innocent children that need to be rescued. There are abused women stuck in a generational pattern that need to be saved.

The lyrics from the song "Reckless Love" by Cory Asbury break me every time I sing them. Singing about Jesus climbing mountains, shining light into darkness, and kicking down walls to come after me gives me chills every time. How I hope and pray that every child, man, and woman who finds themselves in bondage knows that God will come after them. He will kick down walls. He will crash through defenses. He won't stop until everyone is found and restored.

So, what is your role? It could be a lot of things but one thing we can all do—NEED to do—is to pray. We need to pray for the sex industry to be stopped in its tracks. We need to pray for those holding others hostage to be convicted by the Holy Spirit. We need to pray for more people to make bold moves and go to these dark places. We need to pray for a revival.

You see, many people play Satan, but thankfully, there are still many people who like to be on the winning team.

Because Jesus wins.

Now, when I talk about God, my little guy who wanted to play Satan, he tells me that God wins. "He beats Satan, mom. Satan is the bad guy, but God is the best."

God IS the best. And He wins!

Chapter Thirty: Truth

This is the conversation I hear most often in my home right now.

"He's looking at me."
"No, I'm not."
"Yes, you are."
"No, I'm not."
"Yes, you are."
"No, I'm not."
"Yes, you are."

And it goes on and on and on. And it gets louder and louder until everyone is squealing and screaming.

Here's the problem with how that conversation goes. Or at least one problem. Everyone has a version of the truth, but only one of them can be the actual truth. You see, it doesn't matter what we believe; there is still a truth. One of my guys can believe they weren't looking at their brother, but the actual, irrefutable truth is, they were. You can argue it all day long, and they often do, but the facts are in place.

I see this same version of "yes, it is/no, it's not" playing out in society today. Everyone has their own version of the truth. They say, "My truth says . . ." as if that truth is different from yours. Everyone has their own version of what right and wrong are. And if you disagree with their truth, watch out. Screaming and squealing will commence.

I heard an illustration once about this. When you are shopping online and input your credit card number, you must get it all correct. If you are one number off, your purchase will be denied. Close isn't good enough when using a credit card. And close isn't good enough in life.

There is one version of the truth.

God, the Father, is in Heaven.
Jesus is the Son of God.
He was born of a woman and lived on earth as a man, sinless.
He was crucified on the cross, was in the tomb for three days, and rose again.
He is now at the right hand of God.

That is my truth. That is your truth. That is the truth. And we can argue it all we want, but it is still the truth. And as Jesus said, "If you hold to my teaching, you are really my disciples. Then you will know the truth, and the truth will set you free." (*NIV*)

Chapter Thirty-One: Head and Shoulders, Knees and Toes

I always wanted a funny kid. Maybe it's because I'm not funny. Or as a good friend told me, 'But you're not - not funny. I think she meant it as a compliment. I have a sarcastic sense of humor. I like plays on words and one-liners. But I'm not truly a funny person.

Then we had our first set of twins. From the moment 'Baby B' was born, he was funny. They were born early, so his body looked like Gullum, and his face looked like Vizzini from The Princess Bride. Truly he did. And he made the funniest expressions. By the time he could talk, he had comedic timing down. Now, at the age of five, he's hysterical. If you talk to him for two minutes, you will be laughing.

Not only is he funny, but he's also genuinely personable. He compliments people naturally. He's generous with his affection. He doesn't know a stranger. He doesn't care who you are or what you look like. He'll tell you his name, ask yours, ask about your day or where you live. And you will be his new friend.

From the day he was born, I have prayed for this little boy to be full of love and joy. And not "a love" in word only. But a love that moves him to act. When I read through the Gospels and see all the amazing things that Jesus did, I am struck by two things: Jesus saw a need, and then He acted to meet that need.

When I look around, I see needs everywhere. But the greatest need I see is that need for a Savior. Our world is a hurting place. My community is a hurting place. Sometimes my tendency is to see that need and acknowledge it but not act upon it. But that isn't love. Love moves us to act. Love moves us to compassion.

When I look around my world, I see lots of things that I don't like. I'm sure you do as well. We see sin that is a lot like our sin, and it makes us uncomfortable. Or we see sin that is so much worse than ours, and we become judgmental. Or perhaps disgusted. Or self-righteous. We step away from those people because we don't want to associate with them.

Take, for example, homosexuality. Let's say you believe it is wrong. And because you believe it is wrong, and it's something you would never do, you block yourself from anything to do with it. That includes blocking yourself from anyone who lives that lifestyle. Is that the way to live? Is that the way to love? Absolutely not! I'm certainly glad Jesus didn't approach sin that way because the need for the cross would have been a lot different.

One of Jesus's disciples was a tax collector. One of the lowest people of that time. They were thieves, liars, and hated by everyone. But Jesus chose Matthew. Not to just talk to but to walk with.

John 3:16 says that "God so loved the world He sent His one and only Son." (*NIV*) It's not the earth or the universe that He loved. It's us. You. Me. Liars, cheats, adulterers, homosexuals, terrorists . . . you name it, and God meant them. If God loves them, shouldn't we? And if we love them, shouldn't that love move us to act on behalf of them.

We can't run away from the people who have sin we hate. While we don't want to rub shoulders with the sin we are called, I believe, to rub shoulders with the sinner.

What if we ignored all those who are living in the 'bad sins'? (I'm talking here about those who are unsaved and live a lifestyle of what we would consider a 'bad sin.' I do believe you can be saved and still be living in sin, aren't we all that way?) We are saying their sin is too hard for me to love them in. So, I'm going to just let them go to hell. No one would say that, but that's exactly what we are doing. Yes, we pray. But we can't stop there. If I pray for my unsaved gay neighbor and never talk to them or love them, am I really doing my part to bring them to the arms of Jesus? Jesus didn't say pray for the world to know me. He said, "Go therefore and make disciples of all nations . . . teaching them to observe all that I have commanded." (*ESV*)

We are called to go and disciple people. Just because we see something we don't like, or it makes us uncomfortable, does not give us an excuse to remain silent. We need to step into our discomfort and love. Love with actions. "But God demonstrates his own love for us in this: While we were still sinners, Christ died for us." (*NIV*, Romans 5:8)

While you are still an alcoholic, I will love.

While you are still a part of the LGBTQ community, I will love.

While you are still racist, I will love.

While you are still the *thing you hate the most*, I will act. I will love.

My little boy is an inspiration to me. I have seen him love and welcome the unlovable. I have seen him talk to people regardless of race, gender, status, or any other discrimination. His mind has not been formed by the world, and I pray it never will. He walks and plays alongside everyone. Can we all be more like him? Take every prejudiced thought captive. Rub shoulders with those who are not like us. Get on our knees and pray for them. And use our feet to walk through life with them. I think that's when we will see a change around us.

Conclusion: Weight of Glory

Weight. When you see that word, what comes to mind first? Perhaps it's the number on the scale when you step onto it. Maybe it's how many grapes you buy at the store. Or how heavy your suitcase is before traveling. There are so many things that we value by weight.

My smallest baby was 3 pounds 13 ounces, and my biggest was just two pounds heavier at 5 pounds 13 ounces. We saw how two extra pounds of weight made a difference. My biggest baby spent one extra day in the hospital, while my smallest spent 31 days in the NICU. I realize that his stay was not totally dependent on his weight, but his early arrival contributed to his low birth weight.

When something has extra weight, there is more of it—a little extra. When I weigh more, there is a little more of me to be loved. When the weighted blanket goes on the bed, it weighs us down. When you put a full and heavy bag on your shoulder, you feel the weight pulling you down. When it's so very cold outside (something we don't often experience in the south), you put on a heavy coat to feel the weight of warmth on your body.

But sometimes, in life, we don't see weight as a good thing. When we are weighed down by problems, we aren't feeling secure and good. Have you ever felt weighed down by . . .?

- health problems

- loss of a job

- a wayward or disobedient child

- a struggled marriage or other relationship

- financial difficulties

I've felt all of those, and they become heavy. They weigh down your walk, your face, your head, and your spirit.

But here's the thing. In each of those situations, if we give God room to move, we can exchange the weight of this world for the weight of His glory. Did you know the Hebrew word for glory is "kabod," which can find the root meaning to be "weight" or "heaviness"? 2 Corinthians 4:16-18 says, "So we do not lose heart. Though our outer self is wasting away, our inner self is being renewed day by day. For this light momentary affliction is preparing for us an eternal weight of glory beyond all comparison, as we look not to the things that are seen but to the things that are unseen. For the things that are seen are transient, but the things that are unseen are eternal." (*ESV*)

The weight of His glory. The heaviness of His glory. I can see it, sense it, feel it. The weight of the goodness of God. The weight of His love. The weight of His providence in our lives. The weight of HIM. When we experience the weight of His glory, it's so heavy, we can feel it. It's not something we think about or just expect. We know it's there. It is heavy enough to change us, to make us more like Him.

But the weight of His glory is also light. When we focus on His glory instead of our circumstances, our load is lightened.

My husband has congenital heart disease, so there are times when he has immediate and severe health problems. We could find ourselves weighted down in fear or worry, but if we allow the weight of His glory to guide us, there is trust and hope.

When my job was suddenly eliminated, and I found myself being a stay-at-home mom, I didn't know what to think. There was uncertainty about the future—would our finances make it, would I be a good stay-at-home mom, would I like it? But when we trusted in the weight of His glory rather than the weight of a job loss, He showed me that I could prevail even in challenging circumstances.

Many days I find myself disciplining and saying 'no' more than playing and saying 'yes' having four young boys. While they are too young to stray from home with dangerous and illegal activities or to stray from God, I am confronted daily with disobedient children. (I'm sure many of you have been weighed down by even greater challenges with your children than them jumping on the couch.) We could choose to be weighed down by fear for our children and what their future may hold, or we could be weighed down by the glory of God and remember that He loves sour babies more than we do.

There was a season in my marriage where I still loved my husband, but I didn't like him all that much. We found ourselves in patterns of selfishness and negative communication. This could have weighted down our future and our family. But when we allow the weight of His glory into our lives, we can reignite love and joy into our marriages and relationships.

After failed adoptions (think money loss), two successful rounds of embryo adoption (think money hemorrhage), and four kids under the age of two, we found ourselves very far from financial comfort. We could have chosen to dwell on our circumstances and allowed the difference between where we wanted (and at times needed) to be and where we were dragged down. Or we could rest in the weight of His glory and recognize all the small ways that God provided for us and continues to provide.

My hope is that by reading this book, God has been glorified. I'm not perfect—far from it. My kids are not perfect, and I am far from a perfect mom. But . . .

That's the word that changes everything. I am not perfect, **but** God is. I live my life, attempting in the most basic way, to give glory to God. 1 Corinthians 10:31 says, "do all to the glory of God." (*ESV*) So, as I finish writing, can we say we will shrug off the weights of this world? The weights of our inadequacy. The weights of our fears and insecurities. And in return, we can allow ourselves to be weighted by the glory of God.

"Worthy are you, our Lord and God, to receive glory and honor and power, for you created all things, and by your will they existed and were created." (*ESV*, Revelation 4:11)

About the Author

Maggie Adkinson grew up in Pittsburgh, Pennsylvania before relocating to Coastal Georgia where she began her career in Christian Ministry at Compassion Christian Church. Having over a decade of experience as a Children's Pastor she is able to offer a unique view of life, parenting and how the two mix. Now, as a stay-at-home mom to four young boys, Maggie shares this busy stage of life with lots of humor anchored in the knowledge of God's continual presence and purpose in the victories, messes, and mishaps alike. When Maggie is not wrangling her crew, you will find her reading in her hammock, planning trip and travelling, and enjoying time with family and friends. For Little Lives is her first book.

Made in the USA
Coppell, TX
17 November 2021

65942767R00061